My overthinking brain

Sayanora Will Scarlet

BookLeaf Publishing

Presentation by *BookLeaf Publishing*

Web: www.bookleafpub.com

E-mail: info@bookleafpub.com

ISBN: 978-93-95755-76-4

First edition 2022

*To my younger self; in another universe, I
hope you find happiness and love*

ACKNOWLEDGEMENT

Acknowledging my parents, who encouraged me to take up the challenge, and followed up with me every single day regarding the progress.

Thanking everyone who broke my heart and dashed my hope, without whose efforts, this collection wouldn't have been possible.

The next one might sound out of place, but is definitely important. To myself, for staying alive and strong! (because the world doesn't always applaud us, and we need to clap for ourselves and give ourselves a pat on the back when we need it)

Ahalya

Numb mind
Depressed
Just sad?
Or lazy?
Razors are beautiful items in her dreams
That which help ease the pain
Scissors to chop the hair
And tiny blades chip away pieces of soul
That fly into the unknown
In search of its mistress: the true mistress
Not the fake one that held them close
And gave them love when they needed it the
most
The fake mistress sits
Hollow bits to be filled
Like pixels missing from the whole that is her

She tried filling it with water
Water from everyday life
But the formless, tasteless fluid didn't contain
itself
Did not suit her varied tastes
And flowed out of the gaps

Next, she tried filling it with darkness
Darkness from men's abuses

But it filled her entire being with a darkness
beyond description
And she forced it out

Then, she tried filling it with blood
Blood from her bleeding heart
Finally, it fit!
Though a fluid, the viscosity let it keep its place
Dripping now and then, and the blood wasn't
tasteless

Cold and cruel her heart became
Slowly, yet surely
It turned to stone
To stone, to stone
What life can bring it back?
None, I tell you

She has become the bitch in the eyes of the
world
The cold-hearted woman cannot be a wife or
mother
Cannot be the care-taker of a family
And doesn't wish to be one either

Wishes to complete her life in dreary solitude
And hopes to find the strength to do so
Forever her eyes set on stars shining high above

For they led her this far and will lead her
forevermore

Waves hit as hard as she hit rock bottom
day-by-day
Her depression is just as deep as the hunger of
the baby boy
Wailing his eyes out for some bread and soup

The poor can't afford to be depressed, she
thought
Isn't it true?
They've stomachs to fill and no energy to waste
whimpering over some abstract idea called
depression

Her mind tried to wander away from the seeds of
despair
Sown deep into the pits of her maze-like mind
Try digging it out and all you'll find is the dirt
The dirt from the abuses left behind by men
And of all the worldly sins that she has
committed with them

The unwoven tapestry

Threads hanging loose, and
Color of passion,
Currently, peach,
Dripping ever so quietly,
Staining the carpet,
A shade darker than it was.
They grew outrageous,
Only because they were afraid that
The spotless one might be lost soon.
The jasmine made her hair fragrant
Yet, it was starting to attract the flesh flies.
The wounds gave away a stench
That overpowered everything sane and beautiful.
Time passed.
The beauty became the beast.
The foul smelling witch she turned out to be
Blew away all prospects of a forever.

A bloody tale

Scarlet should have been it,
But marmalade stole her heart that day.
The white top of Schiffli lace
Paired with the flowers
Shaded her eyes a tinge of caramel.
To their surprise,
Teardrops the shade of vermilion
Ran down that face,
Unmasking her true self.
Those around screamed in terror.
A vampire was born.

Blue

Cold and sad.
Everything and nothing.
The water and the sky.
Not yin and yang.
Navy blue, royal blue,
Prussian blue and sapphire.
She still remembers
Her iron-heart.
Hell burnt like a fever.
The lifeless heart turned
A shade that shamed the midnight.
Darker and darker,
Until she didn't exist.
Not a soul will miss her,
Not a tear be shed, as
The breeze won't be misted with her presence.

The Story of a Sniff

Lay in bed with fear in my heart.
When next will I hear raised voices from out the door?
For now, I heard mother's soft chant of prayers.
Hope there's a power that gains strength with these prayers,
And answers the tears in her eyes and the fear in mine.

Stuffed with dinner, I rolled around on the bed, playfully, to calm myself down,
And took a casual sniff at my right hand.

Dinner was served earlier;
Rotis with chicken curry.
The smell lingered, the familiar smell of chicken curry as mother always prepared it.
I closed my eyes,
Took a deeper sniff,
And opened my eyes.
Time traveled back, some 11 years,
And I changed back into a Grade 10 student.
Was it real?
It was my old room.
Sniffed my right hand once more,

And found the same familiar smell of the
chicken curry.
I heard mother call,
And stepped out of the room.
Passed a younger, healthier-looking father in the
hall,
Went to the kitchen to find a younger, happier
mother,
"Aren't you going to sleep? Or do you have a lot
of school work to cover?"
I stood staring at her in awe,
Then went and gave her a hug,
"Will check quickly and go to sleep", I replied.
Hurried back to the room ,
And closed the door behind me.
I looked at the mirror.
My geeky hair remained the same, but...
I was too excited about this second chance at
life!
I knew what to do this time around.
Quickly, I opened my diary,
And checked whether I had completed the work.
Once that was done, I went to sleep.
I was even more excited about going back to
school!
I awoke the next day,
Still stuck back in time,
Got dressed in my uniform,
Strutted in it proudly to the bus stop,

On that cold winter morning,
Warmly greeting my dear cousin and friends.
Boarded the bus, and got to school,
But couldn't believe my eyes,
Walking towards 10 G classroom!
Left my bag at a back bench,
Because I knew, this time round,
I had to have fun and make memories.
My classmates seemed a little surprised,
To not find me catching a first bench,
to quickly pop questions at the teacher when she
lectured.
I winked at them,
And twirled around on the spot.
In sometime, I was chit-chattering with everyone
around me,
About everything other than studies;
They were all so surprised!
In a day, it was as though, something had
happened to me.
And wasn't it right?
I had lived my life for 11 years,
And come back to tell the tale; well, not
exactly...
Our assembly began on radio,
And a smile popped on my face.
I knew I had to be a recess radio RJ somehow.
It was always a dream of mine.
Now, that I was more confident,

It would definitely work in my favour.
As the assembly came to a close,
And the first period was announced,
In walked Mrs. Susan Sam,
Ready to battle us with Social Sciences.
Then came Mrs. Ponsi James,
Who couldn't stop referring to the tangents of
triangles.
With a sing-song voice came Mrs. Prema
Pathak,
Lovingly calling us "Mere pyare vachcho"!
And was later replaced by the gorgeous Mrs.
Gladys Samuel,
Yet her monotonous voice coupled with boring
biology,
Slowly put me to sleep.
The rest of the day went in a flow,
With the practical labs, and the teachers walking
in and out,
And the 20-minute recess was the most
memorable,
Because I had missed Nam's tiffin with the aloo
paratha in it.
Time to return home,
And I expectantly looked forward to lunch being
served.
Famished, I reached home,
Only to find mother serving up,
The most aromatic fish biryani;

It almost brought tears to my eyes.
Later, I rolled around on my bed,
And sniffed my right hand;
The familiar smell of fish got me drooling even
after a heavy lunch!
I closed my eyes,
Took a deeper sniff,
And opened my eyes.
Time traveled forward, 11 years,
And I changed back to my 2020 self.
Was it a dream?
Maybe, a poem.

Desperate for love

I am desperate for love
Not just any love
I want to be loved by D

Who's D, you ask?
D is my precious, as Gollum would say
He's the wealth and object of desire of my heart,
but someone I will never call mine

Just to be loved by him
To be held closer to him
To be his
For him to love me above all
For him to, one day, hold my hand
For him to be mine

None of these will even be close to true
Not even in my wildest dreams
Because he is one who'll never belong to me

His umber-coloured almond-shaped eyes draws
me closer to him
His curly-yet-set hair is too good to miss over
the blockade of my office partition

And when his face lifts up and away from his
PUBG life
My heart skips n number of beats I never bother
to count

When in formals, he has a particular aura around
him that I find most difficult to translate into
anything sensible
And it could be popular fact that he makes me
weak in my knees and swoon at the mere sight
of him

To put it simply
He is the stuffing to my chilli-chicken momos
The perfect meat-sauce combination in my
Subway sandwiches
The vanilla whipped-cream topping to my
mixed-fruit pastry
And most importantly, he is the shawarma I
yearn for, but do not deserve

What would I not do to make him mine?
But, the ripping pain within reminds me, once
again, that it'll never be true
The ocean - of cultural and personal differences
- between us will keep us apart forever

Yet, on somedays, when he walks in, sits across
me

And gives me that hint of his most attractive
smile
I find myself lost and being dragged into a
dream world - one where he loves me and makes
me his own!

Sometimes, he cracks his most lame jokes
And I find myself laughing hard, struggling to
catch my breath

On other days, when he's away from his desk,
and as scrum time draws close
My eyes linger near the ODC entrance
Waiting eagerly for him to walk in and crush my
soul!

I still remember the day he smelled like heaven
And as I sat next to him, I was screaming
internally, to be saved!

As girls run behind chocolate boys, here I am!
..running behind a piece of chocolate

When dressed in the royal purple shade to match
my hair clip
Groomed and charming
He seems to be as irresistible as the caramel
pudding I always crave for

He is not the yin to my yang
In fact, we are opposites which could never
complement the other
We could never fit together

Maybe that's why the universe never conspired
to bring him any closer, than he is to me
It would hurt me bad
And the sting would equal that of a direct stab to
the heart with a blunt knife

He, once, proudly spoke about the 'kada' he wore
- of how long he has worn it, and probably, how
close it was to him, I guess
I wish to steal it from him
I want to keep that as a memoir
A constant reminder of how I could never be
with a man like him

What would it be like to hold his hand for a
while?
To feel his warmth and slow-breaths against my
skin
To gape at him as he fell asleep, awe-struck at
his very existence
To shower him with kisses unending
And to pamper him with love unconditional
I can only sigh in sorrow, as they remain wishes
that will never be fulfilled

On a beautiful morning
When my eyes beheld the lovely flowers in the
garden
And memories of you flooded me from within
A huge smile erupted on my face, and a giggle
escaped from my lips unbeknownst to me
The picture-perfect scene would have been
complete if you were around, D

What more do I want to pen down about you?
You've made me laugh
And I love that

When our friends insist on spilling the secrets
regarding my latest crush
I wish I could scream your name to them all
But the fear of earning your disapproval
Holds me back

Even if I am mad about you
The other way round will never hold true
All those gorgeous Jharkhandi girls - I don't
stand a chance!
I burn with jealousy just thinking about how you
would admire those other women
Just the thought of you with another - Lord!
Save me from this pain!

A wise man once asked me to be wary of the
ones who make me feel special because I would
easily hurt at their smallest of mistakes
Well, he wasn't exactly a wise man
It was thambi who said so
But truer words couldn't have been spoken

When you're mad at someone else and you find
yourself on the verge of releasing your wrath
I wish to simply stand next to you
Give you a tight hug
And kiss the bitterness away from your lips

No matter how many times I say it, just doesn't
seem to be sufficient to convey my crazy
feelings for you

Of how I always turn green with envy when you
play along as I tease you with those other girls
Heavens know that I just want to drag all those
others out of the picture
And huddle us together in a perfect frame

Of how, when you stay mad at me, it breaks my
heart
"Please talk to me!", I beg of you, though really
not in that tone
And when your lips break into a smile

Out comes a giggle that almost brings
tears-of-joy to my eyes
Satisfied will my heart be with the gleam in your
eye

Of how you taught me to be strong and
independent
Faster than my own father did
Though it pertained to work, mostly
But, as I loved and yearned for you everyday
Unknowingly, you did also teach me to be strong
in my day-to-day life

Of how you chided me that I knew nothing
about the reality of life
And work was my only strong point:
You were right, D!

I live in a dream world
Where we aren't as far apart as we are now
And..
Birds don't chirp every morning to wake us up,
but a blaring alarm does
We don't jump off to a 'kiss-start', but literally
push each other out of bed to get the other a cup
of tea to 'kick-start' the day
We don't take the leisure of hugging each other
in the kitchen while preparing food, but try to
pack in at least a sandwich or a bowl of cereals

We don't 'kiss-and-make-up' for every fight, but
argue considerably and come to a common page
We don't dress each other up, but literally leave a
mess behind as we rush to office
We don't find time to flirt with each other during
office hours, but end up holding hands at night,
exhausted from the day's work
We don't hug each other to sleep, but definitely,
love falling asleep next to each other
Some weekends, we go to the noisiest parties
On some others, we go on quiet trips
And on some completely lazy weekends, we end
up snuggling next to each other with your
masterpiece: a sumptuous plate of chicken
biryani

On trips alone and solo rides
I often long for your presence
And wonder what it'd be like to have you around
Just the two of us, winds against our ecstatic
faces

On some days, when the thought of you wells up
tears in my eyes
I wish to run up to you, like in the movies
And trust me, my darling, I'd go down on one
knee and profess my love to you!

As my time with you draws to a close

I try to get your attention at all times
I try to enjoy your company
And when you leave sooner than you already do,
the rest of the day just falls apart

On the day you lost a match
I sat next to you, wishing to simply hug you
Even if you didn't need that to comfort you..
Just to feel what it'd have been like to hug my
teddy, D
Instead, as you spoke to someone else, I tried to
tug at the sleeve of your full-sleeved tee
The purpose? Don't ask me because I know not

My days with you are numbered
I count them down with pain
And try to find the courage that slipped past
When disinterest I feigned

In my head, I have myself convinced
That you're angry with the early departure
That you love me more than I love you
That you'll miss me and it'll break your heart
But, none of it is true, D
You're just mad at me for something I'll never
know
You're ruining my last few chances to make
more beautiful memories with you

And you'll never even have second thoughts about
me once I leave

Today, as I sit across and sniff that gorgeous scent off
of you:
The haze of deo with a dash of that fish-like stench of
your sweat
I close my eyes and let the toes curl
Until I imagine your fingers running through your
perfect hair
The temptation is irresistible
And so, I open my eyes and take a sneak-peek
At the little part of your forehead that remains visible
Just musing about how I would love to plant little
pecks of kisses all over them

I break my heart to pieces
Even as you remain oblivious to all these thoughts in
my head
I never stood the chance anyway
I dreamt far and beyond of what I deserved

A precious human like you
Your entitlement to a significant-other:
So beautiful, caring and intelligent
I am like a weed next to the alluring garden of roses
that she is
And you, the little child fascinated by the roses
Trampling upon the weeds and uprooting them with
your bare hands; it hurts, D

From One to the Next

Let us begin with a random thought
One that will lead us to another
But of unconditional love

Promises in a prism
Sunlight streaming through
Promises broken into false hopes

'Hope' is a warm-word
Bitter, rather cold, is 'despair'
Warm or cold, when offered, what will you
choose?

Truth be told, it is cold
Hope, though warm, falsifies existence
And human persistence

Another thought, yet not of love
Mirrors smashed into pieces
Hope and despair fight

Over mountains and through rivers
Flying and flowing
Tiny shards of silver-polished glass

Yet another thought
Of reddened eyes
All tired from crying all night long

And lips so scarlet
The strawberries were put to shame
Watching them overflow

With blood that was poured
Onto her crushed soul
Walking rampant through and through

The next thought
Crushed souls went aside
Discussing what mattered most

In lives of their own
Certain thoughts ruled over their minds
Ego, was it, or simply selfishness?

Thought about it as well
Selfish thoughts entering her mind
"Welcome, welcome", she said

Ruining her life
She realised not
But her life was sketched black

This ending thought

Be it of love in this cold, cold world
Warming to your heart

Raasaave, she will call him
The king who rules her heart
Raasaathi, he'll coo to her nerves

Of love lesser known than
Most famous people in this tiny world of ours
May it shine bright and bring forth

Truth to behold
Joy to the heart
And love, more love to the soul

Sunshine

Oh! Sunshine, so bright, you made me blind.
The sun set, never to return,
Leaving me in darkness.
But, it made no difference,
As my life without luminescence,
Tripped in the deep darkness of loneliness,
Hand held out for relief.
The cold wind blew that night,
A fine attempt by the universe,
To assuage the pain,
That pain of not being able to mirror my
sunshine.
I wait expectantly for the illusion of morn,
For my stone-blind self believes,
That the sunshine that made me blind,
Will surely bring the radiance back to my life.
To reflect your dazzle,
This I dream of;
With you, is this insane-self smitten,
Wishing to be forever yours,

- Moonlight

A parting gift

He lay under the stars
With the frangipani flowers scattered around him.
Thought about the number of times
She could have definitely looked at him;
The least she could have done.

She sat on the toilet floor and sobbed aloud.
The sobs soon turned to heaves and cries;
Refused to come to terms
With a fact as simple as his resignation:
Simple to the world,
Not for her, she reminded herself.

As the two souls pondered
Over their text conversations with each other,
The air around them hung with regret.
The two regret-filled introverts,
Disappointed over their inability
To share their world of stories,
Stuck to being an ordinary pair of acquaintances.

She will never hear his voice,
Never know what he looks like from up close;
Not even know his scent.
Her attempts at closure were failing;
She vowed to never give up.

The dance

As the music was turned on,
Her feet slowly started moving to the rhythm…
She closed her eyes.
She felt his presence around her;
So she lifted her arms
Wrapped it around his neck
And hung onto him.
They moved to the beats,
Even their breaths in-sync.
He pulled her closer to him,
Ever so lightly.
She rested her head against his chest
Hugging him by now.
Their feet in constant motion;
The song comes to a closure —
She opens her eyes
To return to her life full of void.

The confused little soul

Love bloomed to the beat of Pasoori
But just in her heart.
To him, she was just another passer-by.
A friend, maybe
Nothing more.

Her yearning; to spend more time with him
His; beyond her.

She felt that he was perfection defined
Put him on a pedestal
Adored him.
Even his sweat was something she found
attractive.
His tall, dark, handsome self
Needn't mention, swept her off her feet.

It was their third meeting.
Puffing in that smoke together
The cannabis took them to another world.
The sound of water and air
Rushed through their ears.
She seduced him
Cuz that's all she knew.
And he was an angel that fell for it.

He held her with love that night.
She felt his caress
Similar to that of an angel's touch.
His kisses covered every inch of her.
Her joy knew no bounds.
She felt an ecstasy like never before.

When he left the next morn
Her heart sunk in the ocean.
Her confused little soul didn't know
Whether to be excited about the butterflies in her
stomach
Or be sad about it all.

This confused little soul
Knew she'd be hurting herself
Deeper than all she had gone through
If she let him stay.

Her choice defining her future;
She decided to let him go.

Hold me close forever, she wished
Yet it remained a dream
For the rest of her life.

The bitter truth

In coloured bubbles, I see
Me and you, sitting together
Hand in hand,
Having a little conversation
About a future, that seems
Far and beyond, as in a dream.

We talk for eternity, or so
That's how it seems.

And then all of a sudden,
The bubble bursts
And everything nice and good
Disappears into thin air.

And as I get to think about it,
Life is amazing as we know it.
Dreams motivating us so,
Both wild and imaginary,
Both small and real,
Yet we yearn to fulfill it,
Though sometimes we know it not to be so.

A random man

The tall wonder — that's what I'd like to call
him…
One day at lunch, I felt his piercing stare
through my skin.
As he sat at the table across mine,
And his girlfriends giggled at my funny
appearance,
I felt the blood rush to my cheeks…
And, then, he stood up to show-off
His 6-something-foot self.
I felt a gasp of awe escape me,
And the beats of my heart resounded as thuds
To coincide with every move of his…
Today, as I saw him dressed in that smooth black
shirt,
My monster lingered at the surface of my mask,
Hoping to, one day, experience all that lay
beneath the surface.

Driven crazy

I am afraid of forgetting his face, his smile,
The laugh that made my knees weak.
I forgot to notice his hands.
Sad to say, they'll never hold me as I dreamt.
I recollect his voice, his accent;
I want to preserve them with embalming fluids.
Stay in my memories, at least;
I really don't want to lose that about you, as
well!
You ran me down with your insanity,
And left without saving me…

The storm

As I sat on the cold ground
And lit up my cigarette,
Teardrops fell out of my eyes.
All on a sudden, you were standing
Right in front of me.
I got up, feet staggering
And looked into your eyes,
As they read every emotion that ran within me.
You stood there with your hands held out for me.
I yearned for you to wipe away my tears and so,
I walked towards you, or rather
An illusion of you,
As my hallucination of you
Disappeared in the cloud of smoke
From my cigarettes and left me, once again,
To drown in my ocean of tears.

Love or lust?

He called me moonlight;
I could never say whether he meant it.
My hormones let loose my 'cheesiness',
And in return, I called him sunshine.
On somedays, he called me dreamboat;
Never could say whether he did so out of
realization,
Or just another fancy term he came across in the
movies.
But for every name that he gave me,
Love exploded exponentially.
I fell in love with both the mask and the
monster,
And wished for the two to unite.

We are alone

The lonely road winds through the forest.
Two souls cross paths.
The road will never feel so alone, as at that
moment,
When the bubbles around them moulted,
A new bubble to encapsulate them together;
Floats with them to a far-off land.
Imagination will repeat itself,
Every time two souls cross a lonely path…

Somebody else's man

I turned to the left,
Only to be awe-struck by the man who sat on the
bench there,
And, as usual, my eyes looked for either of those
signs which marked him as 'forbidden'.
Then, my eyes cast its sight on that which tore
my heart to pieces.
His woman came and sat next to him,
A lady so beautiful that her mere presence
Was enough to drag my confidence to the
bottom of Mariana's Trench.
As they sat together, holding hands,
The rush of jealousy that ran through me was
quite unfamiliar.
Yes, I have been jealous before; just never of
somebody else's man...

Roy

The first time I heard that voice,
I warned myself not to turn around and find the
man with that voice.
When I finally found the source of that purrrr...it
was surprisingly scary.
The handsome Bengali that was the object of my
nightmares,
Appeared in front of me.
He was the perfectly baked brown bread.
He never looked perfect in pictures,
And was definitely one to be noticed in-person.
Something hit me hard on my senses everytime I
tried to speak to him.
I found them asking me to talk sense, never
nonsense,
Hoping that I'd never come across as the idiot
yapping no-sense.
As I got to know him better,
It became even more difficult to resist him.
The average Bengali loves fish - my weakpoint,
and football - a game I fancied, probably a bit
too much
This one, I'm yet to find his love for 'machher',
But his love of football is definitely something I
find attractive.

His toned-self with that little pout of a tummy -
a sure-shot way to my heart;
How did that coincide with him?

Two sides to a coin

He wasn't a heartbreaker.
Justification?
He squiggled his way through the tiny pores.
Took out all the trash within;
Or so he claimed.
In the process, he coded in a virus,
The ends of which kept spreading.
And before it blew out of proportion,
He escaped for dear life.

As for her, there is no looking back.
Slowly dreading the doom that awaits her.
As moments of life flash slowly before her eyes,
It is as though the knell of death has been rung,
And the time to partake in an angel's funeral has
come.

The doubt? None.
The world condemned her,
For she was nothing but a whore.

Her story? Too quiet.
A stereo blasted white noise.
She could only think of painting it.
But a life devoid of colours

Was of no help to her.
Swept the dust of depression
Below the rug of happiness.
Called up on karma because
Revenge was all she wanted.

Young and lost

Days before I turn 17,
I realize that I haven't grown up with time.
Thinking of good old life
And of silly mistakes I've made in life.
Every time I made a decision,
I took a challenge upon myself;
To do or die was basically all it was about.
The recent changes, the recent blows,
All unacceptable yet,
According to laws of nature, has to be so.
As I pen my thoughts on paper,
I take a look at 18 girls and 5 boys,
All aspiring to be doctors and engineers,
And realizing I'm such a fool
To have thought I could become one, too;
Having a brain that does not match
Even a rattlesnake's!